BRILLIANT PEOPLE, BIG IDEAS

Written by
Rebecca Phillips-Bartlett

TRANSPORT

BookLife
PUBLISHING

©2023
BookLife Publishing Ltd.
King's Lynn, Norfolk
PE30 4LS, UK

All rights reserved.
Printed in China.

A catalogue record for this book is available from the British Library.

HB ISBN: 978-1-80505-009-4
PB ISBN: 978-1-80505-379-8

Written by:
Rebecca Phillips-Bartlett

Edited by:
Kirsty Holmes

Designed by:
Isabella Croker

FSC
www.fsc.org
MIX
Paper from responsible sources
FSC® C113515

All facts, statistics, web addresses and URLs in this book were verified as valid and accurate at time of writing.
No responsibility for any changes to external websites or references can be accepted by either the author or publisher.

Image Credits

All images are courtesy of Shutterstock.com, unless otherwise specified. With thanks to Getty Images, Thinkstock Photo and iStockphoto.

Recurring images – Andrew Rybalko, cosmaa, andromina, P-fotography, Mark Rademaker, IGORdeyka. Cover – Andrew Rybalko, dimair, cosmaa, andromina, P-fotography. 2–3 – Andrew Rybalko. 4–5 – IGORdeyka, Macrovector, Krakenimages.com. 6–7 – Naci Yavuz, Fourvierolim. 8–9 – Looper, Everett Collection, Serg_Zavyalov_photo. 10–11 – Lesseps, Magnus Manske, Irina Qiwi, AntiDeviL, J J Osuna Caballero. 12–13 – Flash Vector, Wiki LIC, klyaksun. 14–15 – shako, PixelSquid3d, Ann in the uk, Scewing. 16–17 – Nesnad, Chereliss, Foto-Ruhrgebiet, Flash Vector. 18–19 – In-Finity, Real Vector, Valentina Sabelskaia. 20–21 – BlueBreezeWiki, Montbarrey, Morphart Creation, Panda Vector, PK Designs, ideyweb, Andrey Korzun. 22–23 – topseller.

Contents

Page 4	Big Ideas
Page 6	The Montgolfier Brothers
Page 8	Richard Trevithick
Page 10	Karl Drais
Page 12	Mary Anderson
Page 14	The Wright Brothers
Page 16	Garrett Morgan
Page 18	Nils Bohlin
Page 20	The Hall of Fame
Page 22	All You Need Is an Idea!
Page 24	Glossary and Index

Words that look like this can be found in the glossary on page 24.

Big Ideas

We travel all the time. We can ride to school on our bikes, or even fly across the world on holiday. Did you know that none of this used to be possible?

Now, travelling is easy. It took some brilliant people with some very big ideas to make this happen. These people spotted problems with how we travelled, and <u>invented</u> new ways to get around.

What is your favourite way to get around?

5

The Montgolfier Brothers

We are the Montgolfier brothers. We wanted to be able to fly!

1740–1810
Joseph-Michel Montgolfier

1745–1799
Jacques-Étienne Montgolfier

Hot Air Balloons

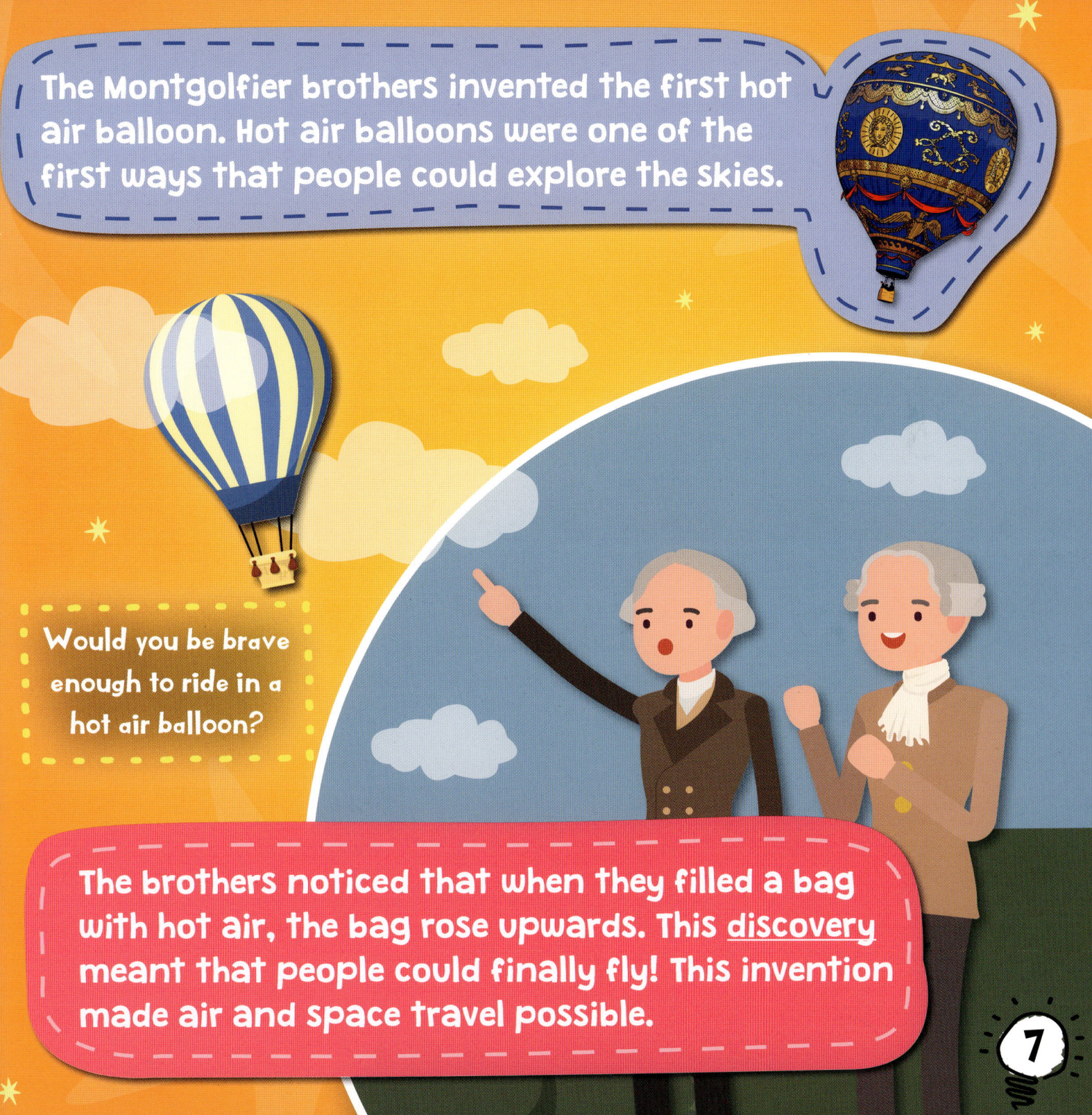

Richard Trevithick

I am Richard Trevithick. Horses are so slow and weak!

1771–1833

Steam Trains

Richard Trevithick wanted a better way of moving heavy coal and iron. So, he invented the steam train. At first, his train was too heavy for the rails. It took a long time for his invention to work properly.

Have you ever been on a train?

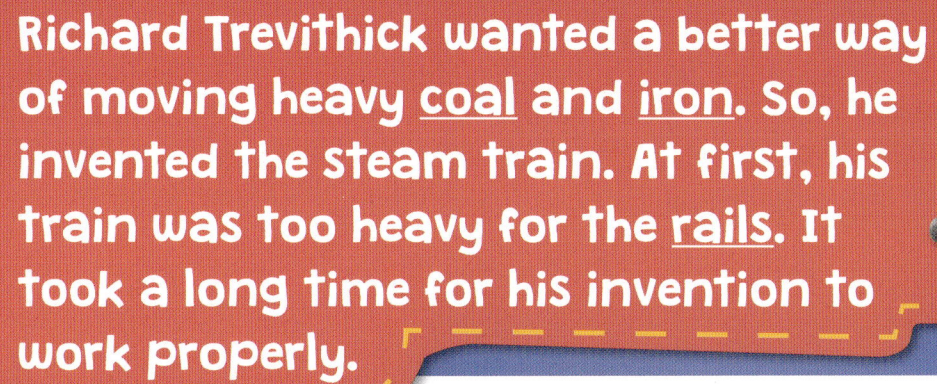

Trevithick's train was nicknamed the Puffer. It got this name because, as it moved, it made big clouds of steam, like a puffing dragon.

Karl Drais

I am Karl Drais. There are not many horses around at the moment. How will we get around?

1785–1851

Bicycles

Mary Anderson

1866–1953

> I am Mary Anderson. My drivers keep stopping to clear their windows. There must be a way of cleaning car windows without stopping...

Windscreen Wipers

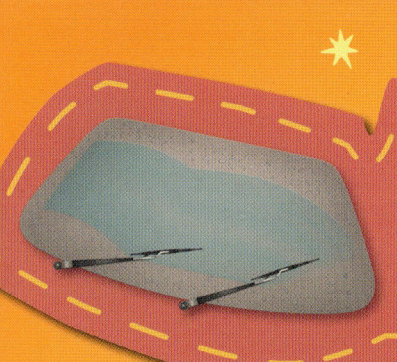

Mary Anderson invented windscreen wipers. Windscreen wipers sweep the windows clean so the driver doesn't have to do it themselves.

What is the weirdest thing you have seen out of the car window?

Every car today has windscreen wipers. Windscreen wipers make driving much safer. It is much harder to drive when you cannot see where you are going!

The Wright Brothers

Wilbur Wright
1867–1912

Orville Wright
1871–1948

We are the Wright brothers. We loved playing with a flying toy as children. Imagine if we could make a real-life flying machine...

Aeroplanes

The Wright brothers invented, built and flew the first <u>engine-powered</u> aeroplane.

Have you ever been on an aeroplane? How long was your flight?

The first flight took place in 1903. This flight only lasted a few seconds, but they kept working on it, and created planes that could fly farther and for longer.

Garrett Morgan

1877–1963

I am Garrett Morgan. Roads are very busy nowadays! There must be a way to stop cars from bumping into each other all the time.

Traffic Signals

Nils Bohlin

"I am Nils Bohlin. Most cars do not have seatbelts. This does not seem very safe!"

1920–2002

Seatbelts

18

Nils Bohlin invented seatbelts like we use today. Before Bohlin's invention, only some cars had seatbelts, and the seatbelts had many problems.

It took many years for Bohlin's invention to become popular. People were not used to wearing seatbelts and did not understand why they should start using them. His invention has saved millions of lives.

Who reminds you to wear your seatbelt?

The Hall of Fame

Here are some more brilliant people who deserve a place in our Hall of Fame.

Claude de Jouffroy d'Abbans

1751-1832

Claude de Jouffroy d'Abbans invented steamboats. This made it much easier to travel long distances across the ocean.

Karl Friedrich Benz

1844-1929

It took many brilliant people to invent the cars we use today. Karl Friedrich Benz was one of these people. He came up with a new kind of engine that we still use today.

Sergei Korolev

1907-1966

Sergei Korolev invented many amazing spaceships. He invented the spaceship which sent the first animals and humans into space!

All You Need Is an Idea!

From hot air balloons to seatbelts, everything had to be invented. The people who came up with these inventions are brilliant. Their inventions all started with a big idea!

These inventors were trying to solve a problem. Travelling was too slow, cost too much money or was not very safe. Not only did these inventors solve these problems, but they have changed the way we travel hundreds of years later!

What would you invent to make travelling better?

Glossary

coal	a kind of rock that is found under ground and used for fuel
discovery	something that has been found out about something
engine-powered	something that uses a machine called an engine to make it work
invented	came up with something new
iron	a heavy metal which is found under ground
pedals	levers that you move with your foot to make something work, such as a bike's pedals
rails	steel bars that make tracks for vehicles with wheels

Index

aeroplanes 14–15
bicycles 4, 10–11
cars 12–13, 16, 18–19, 21
dragons 9
horses 8, 10
hot air balloons 6–7, 22
seatbelts 18–19, 22
spaceships 21
steam trains 8–9
steamboats 20
traffic signals 16–17
windscreen wipers 12–13